GW00771589

# *Papercuts*

## Bernadette Cremin

**salmon**poetry

Published in 2015 by
Salmon Poetry
Cliffs of Moher, County Clare, Ireland
Website: www.salmonpoetry.com
Email: info@salmonpoetry.com

Copyright © Bernadette Cremin, 2015

ISBN 978-1-910669-05-1

All rights reserved. No part of this publication may be reproduced or transmitted
in any form or by any means, electronic or mechanical, including photography,
recording, or any information storage or retrieval system, without permission in
writing from the publisher. The book is sold subject to the condition that it shall
not, by way of trade or otherwise, be lent, resold or otherwise circulated without
the publisher's prior consent in any form of binding or cover other than that in
which it is published and without a similar condition, including this condition,
being imposed on the subsequent purchaser.

COVER PHOTOGRAPHY: *Jessie Lendennie*
COVER DESIGN & TYPESETTING: *Siobhán Hutson*
*Printed in Ireland by Sprint Print*

*To You, the Reader*

# Acknowledgments

Acknowledgments are due to the publishers of Bernadette Cremin's previous collections, in which many of the poems in this book first appeared:

*Perfect Mess* (UK: Biscuit Publishing, 2006)

*Speechless* (UK: Waterloo Press, 2007)

*Miming Silence* (UK: Waterloo Press, 2009)

*Loose Ends* (USA, Pasadena, Red Hen Press, 2012)

# CONTENTS

# ACHE

The clinic sweet nurse said that focus
would lend me perspective but knew
that I could quote that text book too.

Apologising for the 'sharp scratch'
she released the black elastic tourniquet
and bled another needle of me out.

I said I liked her brave new haircut,
a bleached crop that gifted her
ballerina cheekbones

in some attempt to put her at ease,
to let her know that it had stopped
hurting me long before she was born.

I watched her sift her pretty head
for a compliment to hand me back
but one day she'll understand

sometimes it's kinder to just smile.

# AFTER DARK

Crows land on my eyelids,
stagger jagged tracks toward
my lipstick line and peck.

The mirror takes me hostage
as morning surveys the carnage,
my laughter has turned traitor.

Each smile leaves a tangled clue
to whom this mouth has tasted,
words it has kissed and chewed.

Deep crevices, rat tail thick
leave trails of days and nights,
crawling down my cheeks.

Age is an anxious art,
a creased map of flesh and skin —
the bubble that blunts the pin.

# ALBINO

Teresa consumed me

(not in the same way as Sister Martha's tash,
each others' tits, snoggin' or even Top of The Pops)

but that summer curiosity wore me like lovesickness
as I became slowly obsessed with the new girl, Teresa.

Sister Patricia always hid her in well intended corners
to protect her soft eyes from sunlight like a thin plant.

She was exempt from outdoor sport without a note
which made Helen Mc Keever angrier than maths.

I remember how mad I got the day that Declan joked
that she caught it from a rabbit and nicknamed her 'Lettuce'.

I never did believe her excuses when I invited her to drool
over the lads football practice and swap makeup and gossip with us.

I once sat behind her in French, transfixed by the opaque ponytail,
pale and shy as an ivory bride tied by a slim lemon ribbon

and what a blow to the gut it was when Sister Dympna explained
that the pop-star-dark glasses she was allowed to wear in class

were nothing to do with being a Marc Bolan fan, but rather they
were like jailers who locked her rose tinted vision in.

# ANON

He's a saturated rain cloud
massaging the flood.

He stalks shadows round corners,
carves his odour into the dark.

His eyes are keen as sex
and I imagine him growing erect

winding his tongue around itself
when he jerks-off in public toilets.

His slit-lips stretch across his face
slash-thin as the greasy ponytails

I watch scoring heroin in the dead-
electric high street as rush hour begins.

I feel sad for this man,
locked into his counterfeit grin

I can see he's terrified as bone china,
his failure to forge the airbrushed smiles

and sun kissed lifestyles that sneer
at him from between the tacky ads

for discreet sex, Virgin internet,
Sky, iPods and Wiis,

hush-safe abortions and The Samaritans
that wink at him on the Brixton tube.

He is a black-booted toothache,
grey plasticine pushed down the crack.

I feel a sad
for this man.

# ARTWORK

The sun-punished landscape
takes up too much space
like the woman who mumbles
on the rush hour bus.

The adolescent sky fades
into the institutional blue dayroom
where parents come at weekends
to rock their twisted children.

In the kitchen above the bread bin
between a health and hygiene certificate
and Times New Roman note that reads:
Please Turn Kettle Off At Wall

a surreal portrait sulks like an oily teenager,
another staff masterpiece
from a last chance night class
unframed, unsigned.

# BIRTH

is the only party
you are invited
to gatecrash

allowed
to howl yourself
inside out

where custody is given
to gravity and oxygen
the moment when

innocence turns
its head and senses
explore rawness.

It's where you end up
before you start
like a dice thrown

at the dark for a life
that will wear you,
the day you begin,

a name and date
printed on the certificate
that proves you exist.

# BLACK

Fumbling for keys in a black patent bag —

the only one I have with matching heels.
I bought them in the sales, a size too small,
a little too high, half price.

I find a damp handkerchief, a cough drop,
a broken string of plastic pearls,
a scrunch of bus tickets, my new red purse.

The host of sympathy cards and tags
that I picked from the bouquets and wreathes
now left to death at the head of your grave.

But you are in my safe keeping drawer —
in a heat sealed transparent forensic bag.
Your body is in God's custody, but to me

you are the pewter kidney shaped lighter
that I had engraved for you with love
to wrap in the palm of your hand.

The stainless steel comb,
bay rum and dandruff
stuck between its teeth —

reminds me of the bald patch
our son Kevin has inherited
with your lisp and awkward jaw.

Your tobacco stained dentures,
an incisor chipped on a humbug
on a day trip to Clacton,

your stopped watch, wedding band
and the St Christopher that you drove
into black ice.

# BLIND LION

Jean groomed my wedding
into a militia of plan Bs
that anticipated creases, sticky-
fingers, raised eyebrows, tears.

She preyed on the only promise
I'll ever make, like a blind lion
in an abattoir, honed me into
whale bones, an impossible waist,

an ivory silk coffin of shallow breaths —

My bespoke sister chose my bouquet,
a calligraphy of swollen yellows
and as usual was followed everywhere
by glances and her chorus of malt curls.

My hapless locks were bribed by a tiara
and a pinch of silver glitter by a timid
Susan — someone with naked fingers
Jean had sniffed off the internet.

Jean ushered me like a clumsy puppy
into tamed poses with the same strangers
I only ever meet in photos, who sometimes
share a surname, a hint of jaw line.

My smile fevered on numb lipstick
like a trapeze artiste poised, anticipating...
the flash, that smack in the back of my eye
as the paid stranger with ideal teeth

bit smiles out of me...

Confetti is a pretty bomb,
a chaotic tissue of hearts
blown across tarmac,
whispered into corners,

airless places.

# BRIGHT SATURDAY

Spring unwinds
as a hush of buttercups
curtsy in the tiny breeze

then the soft punch
of jasmine takes my mind
by the hand back to May 1973.

I was a ponytail and freckles
my dress a wash of bluebells
that bright Saturday.

That bright Saturday
Mr Jim didn't come home
from work

That bright Saturday that
peeled his wife's smile off
and she stopped…

baking misshapes
pushing red sweets
through the broken fence.

That bright Saturday
her garden began to grow
so slowly into lonely

a death-scape of dandelion heads
incestuous weeds and an apple tree
that surrendered into a buckled fist

a vice of thistles spread
like disease round the ankles
of her backcombed roses.

barbs and thorns clung
like lunatics to the legs
of her gloss-white beehive.

In later years I dared myself
to stand too close to it, pressed
my head against buzzing wood,

drenched in its malicious music.
That is where I learned the sound
of stings breeding

and how to decipher the bizarre
maps that trapped wings beat
when trying to escape the dark.

The fascination with threat
that still keeps me awake
when the night doesn't fit.

# BROKEN BIRD

His pulse drags
its club foot
across the screen:
a broken bird flying
east in a green sky.

The monitor hiccups
he dribbles and grunts
smothers in toxic sleep
while his brain leaks
provocatively.

Under fluorescence
I button up against expected
frost and watch him thaw
in October's leftover sun
while headless prayers hang

around him like orphans and
I need
the way he used to look back at me
I wish...
I were an egg in the palm of his hand.

# CARAMEL COCOA CLUB

Nan was livid as vinegar
whenever she smelled

the kaleidoscope of butterflies
dance around my perfume

or heard the sapphire Capri
that used to call for me

to go run like a slut
to party with hot snow

in the seamless corridors
of the Caramel Cocoa Club

where muscular baselines
melted me into soft knots

and incisor smiles
convinced me to drink

cocktails that matched my eyes
and a cunning tongue

with matador hips hid
his dirty secrets in me.

# CAVEAT

Christmas was
the white liar

that convinced me
to invite a party

to this waste of faces
that spilled drink

and dropped ash
on my carpet

left stains
to look up skirts

while the ceiling
counted bald spots

blossoming
like shy moons.

I knew his excuse
was a best friend's advice

when he left
a too polite kiss

and eloped alone
Cinderella-early.

I watched his slow car
from an upstairs window

ice on the drive
while the party

screamed like a child
tugging at the hem

of a bruised dress.

# CELIA

Celia keeps the bits
of manicure sets
that no one understands

a cheap bottle of perfume
rusted by the sun
she's accidentally let in

a buckled postcard from Paris
signed by a dramatic hand
and three kisses

rolls nervous chewing-gum
in ash with matchsticks
wears pinching patent shoes

that she didn't choose and sits
catatonic as porcelain
so close to the window.

Celia has spent herself
dissecting the trivial street
through drizzle blistered glass

her silhouette is a cut
out of sour cloud
her shadow a spill

under the ugly furniture
that she didn't choose.
Her own hostage

in a magnolia room
that lets the cold in
when no one is looking.

# CHARADE

Kate visits Tom on Fridays after work
chit-chats to the familiar ward staff
then waits in the polite dayroom
for a pastel uniform to wheel him in.

Tom sits opposite, drools and grunts
like selfish sex and the charade begins:
Kate mimes her week unconvincingly
while Tom stares into somewhere else.

They don't talk since the stroke
bit his tongue out and burst his head
like a black and red feathered pillow
leaving love to struggle, a choking fish.

# CHERRY PINK

Seagulls graze on sky above the nursery,
clouds yawn and stretch apricot and violet
into powder blue and china white. Night

is late. In the playground a swing sits still,
overlooked by a squad of toys that squat
on the sill poking fun at the empty yard.

Cherry pink chalk matchstick men march
across tarmac, the wooden horse needs
a child on its back, a lick of paint. Night

is late. It's the anniversary of Mr Perry's
death. They found him a year ago today
swinging like lead from his garage roof

in a zero of rope. The news was translated
for the kids by parents reduced to innocence
and a rash of gossip spread across the tabloids

before anyone said a word. I remembered
the date on the bus, got off at the wrong stop
to come and feed the birds.

# CLAUDETTE

I met Claudette at a poetry group
of lilac shampoo and sets, dress rings
lavender and *Blue Grass* eau de toilette.

In spite of the years that lived between us,
our clashing accents and bank balances.
We fit. Claudette, was a random blessing.

Her sling-backed fascination was reckless:
'So, tell me darling, what's he like in bed?
Has he got a good job darling; big house?
For Christ's sake darling please, at least a wife?'

She quizzed me into giggling snorts
coaxed me teased me into a seamless blush
while we feasted on smoked salmon paté
and sherry, playing backgammon and chess

(decadent damsels in her attic-flat).
She licked her lips whenever I fed her
my secondhand kisses like bulging grapes,
and I savoured her wise, quirky advice,
her recollected life, romance, heartache,
the lovers, the deaths, the wars; poetry.

I need to think our schoolgirl banter helped
to bevel the cancer that nibbled her spine
like a conscience's rat. Her dark ache.

Toward the end I bought her acid drops,
slices of ripe pineapple wrapped in foil
to try and stave the blunt drug that suckled
the spit and merciless humour from her.

I could see when she was ready to leave,
she simply stopped wearing lipstick one day.
The tears budded when I kissed her goodbye
in the hospice and bloomed behind my eyes
like impatient lemons waiting to burst
as the bus passed her flat on my way home.

# COBWEBS

I hate this wallpaper, bouts of flowers
that pout like un-dusted whores.
Roses remind of excuses, guilt.

We planned to redecorate
once upon a long time ago,
even discussed colours,

patterns, hues, when we understood
the subtleties that breathed between us –
the reassurance of contradiction.

You compliment the buttons on my dress,
feign interest in my day like a neighbour
and I pretend to Thank You Kindly.

I offer to make tea and think of biscuits
like a proper wife but the only spark
left between us are the mindless goldfish

that plait water round a plastic cactus
for hours and hours
and...

the suicidal bubbles throwing themselves
at the oxygen that preys on the surface
as they reach for the sky.

The only signs of life left are wilting buds,
a mess of fish dying for breath,
and cobwebs.

# COINCIDENCE

I had a full English breakfast
with a Millwall supporter,

he had a Union Jack tattooed
across his back, blade to blade.

We had chatted each other up
in a Travelodge bar in Coventry.

He made me laugh like a drain
and had eyes like Jesus

in the painting that used to hang
above my nan's mantlepiece

in a gilt frame from a jumble sale
between a crucifix and Virgin Mary.

We invited the glamour-model
with a chip on her shoulder

to make up the crowd,
but she stained the white towels

and smeared the bathroom tiles
with fake tan and broke a nail.

We were all from London
and loved the peep show

but each others' taste in music
and reasons for being in Coventry

overnight were very different.
I had come to read at a poetry gig,

he was a Mc Alpines fusilier
here to extend the reception desk

and she had come to meet her dad
for the first time since he left

her mum eight months pregnant.
She'd found him on the internet

Googling amateur photographers
*out of town*.

# CRAFT

He crafts argument
like fresh scissors

precise and cautious
as the letter v

dovetails each syllable
until it fits exactly.

She sits in the curfew
of skirting boards

listening to the livid sun
scream in through windows.

The garden has become a view
touched through gloves

a massacre of tulips
and tight-lipped carnations

(the vase waits on the top shelf
obedient as dust)

while she learns to count clouds
how to mend the hem

where to find a petrol green
butterfly wing in a bruise

and how to fold everything
perfectly in half.

# CREASE

I was taught how to knit
before my hands
could hold themselves

told how to fool and fumble
with needles and wool until
I learnt the purpose of a jumper

the perfect fit...
how to sit straight
and keep a crease quiet.

# DAZED ANGEL

Her boiled voice gargles
wrong answers to his crossword clues
he feeds her mashed banana
with a plastic spoon

picks out soft centres
peels fruit with a patient blade
tidies her bedside cabinet
every evening before he leaves.

He invents gossip and well wishes
from neighbours who never visit
and repeats the same over-animated tale
about a cat she can't remember since

her head collapsed.

        But when he wheels her
        to November bruised windows
        I am not brave enough for words
        to describe their crooked silhouette:

        wrapped in the scarf of starlings
        that carves its path toward West Pier
        her hand in his, a broken wing
        that hangs between them.

A dazed angel.

# DISLOCATED

She abandoned her desk
to walk in the park
watch the life she dislocated

when the past was on her side,
before she sold her ticket home
to buy crusts for the birds.

She likes this naive season best
before the snowdrops melt,
tulips hang their heads in shame

and the dairy cool breeze
chases its tail through the trees,
stirring great globes of leaves

like schools of nervous fish.
The months before summer
turns, cunning as tobacco.

She waited, unplugged and thin
in a room with a starched view
for him to return her calls but

he mislaid a promise to visit
somewhere between the lines
in a letter she still reads aloud.

# DIVAS

Every weekend we waited
for the milk train from Euston,
broken chocolate machines,
we read graffiti backwards
on corrugated shop fronts
our stockings danced
into ladders and ash

and…

Every weekend he waited,
Bob the Busker with Bob the Dog,
coppers in a patchwork bowler
his saxophone bruised music
that curled my gut like sex
and melancholic lyrics sung
too beautifully out of tune.

# ELAINE

Elaine advocates the hygienic benefit of stockings.

She always compliments homemade cake
and is allergic to strawberries.

Every second Monday she visits Kirby Central library
to renew her spinster aunt's romantic paperbacks.

Elaine buys her books direct from an independent press
that specialise in French novelettes with casual titles.

She drives a pine fresh fiesta with cream interior and
forbids her sticky niece to sit in the backseat.

She wears tortoise shell varifocals, a pale cologne
and a silver band on the ring finger of her right hand.

She is shy breasted, takes her wafer waist for granted
and has climbed to middle management without heels.

She attends a fictitious night class in contemporary art
to escape the Friday night drink after work

and finds that parties give her migraines around ten thirty
she apologises too convincingly then takes the longest route home

with Classic FM or Janis Joplin depending on the moon.

# FLIRT

Gregg picks up butts
because he needs to flirt
with dirty things

he is a back door ajar,
uneasy in kitchens at parties
or the same room as Elvis.

He licks inanimate objects,
textures and unexpected flavours
prove he is here, still in the room,

that he hasn't been butchered
by the spiteful nightmare
that rips his sleep into rags

like a wet baby.

# FOR THE KIDS

We sat on the wrong side of sympathy

as Dr Scott's manicured words
outlined the shadow that has crawled
around your lung like spiteful ivy
since last autumn.

For the last time we faced
that painting in her consulting room:
'Mountain' (oil on canvas). Abstract.
Signed in a contrived hand, underlined.

For a moment truth made the view bigger.
Outside, London was still happening,
red, amber, green.
Brixton was planning its tea.

You fussed with your cuff like a truant
as the diagnosis was disguised
in plain English for us to take home
to the kids, a gift-wrapped grenade.

Forever gracious you offered to drive
knowing I am petrified of twilight.
We sat, gridlocked, then as if it didn't matter
you leant forward, let a violin out of the radio.

We pulled into the drive, parked.
Chloe's bike was still against the shed
where yesterday had left it.
Now is where the end begins:

I'll start to collect your silhouettes,
fingerprints left on glass and plastic,
your discarded shadows, left-over profiles
and rough sketches I'll never show you

for the portrait I'll paint,
David (oil on canvas). Abstract.
To hang at that sly angle
only you would understand.

# FRUIT FOR RUMOURS

I sit on the cracked plastic swing
in a playground I found

a few months ago
in a bus window:

half swing, half not
and watch evening

sign its senile will
in lard coloured clouds

that gang up like cancer
overhead.

The threat of rain is exhausting
I want to still smoke.

I didn't notice tea time
empty the climbing frame,

lose its mitten in the grass,
leave the hopscotch-scuffed tarmac

behind till tomorrow after school.
I sit, half swing, half not

and listen to sounds knit
like skin healing.

A woman alone
in a dim playground

I have become
fruit for rumours.

# GRAHAM'S WIFE

Over the years she's learned to ignore him
sniffing through the recycling

checking for her little mistakes, desperate
for clues to how she spends her days.

Now she always leaves an unrinsed tin
or two and a few unsorted magazines

to justify his complaints
and never mentions the hours he wastes

tinkering in the shed after work.
The endless trimming and preening

loose ends off the garden.

# GROWING PAINS

Silence was
the lullaby you left
to keep Susan awake.

She wasted her teenage
hunting for the reason
in your record collection

she untangled Joy Division,
Two-Tone and Ska until
anorexia finally broke her.

She unstitched each lyric
gnawed every chorus and verse
punished herself like a thin dog

because you left her the red thing
that any glass shape can cut
out of a wrist and…

I hope you had time to panic properly
time to regret the mess you left
for your mother to find

time to watch your soft pulse
throb like love-sex into the warm bath
you drew like a Hollywood cliché.

I hope you had time to panic properly.

See now I just remember you
as the one with fat fingers
that Susan even bothered to kiss

another would-be local hero
that us hungry girls fell in love with
(until our periods started)

but I never will forget your dad
in my dad's chair drinking whiskey
asking me to write your eulogy

because I write poetry
and wouldn't let him down
so it was for him alone

that I took a filthy drug at your funeral
so that I was capable to stand at the altar
to tell lies for your mother

to a too young congregation
that stood in their older brothers' suits
smart shoes and awkward black ties

casting their aimless prayers into the sky
while I begged God for a selfish frost
to chew the football pitch you ran across
every fucking Sunday.

# GUN

Come on Kate, I want to show you something
in a mauve window display. She agrees,
hesitantly, but I notice that she
has started stepping on the cracks again.
We walk, I ask her to spell marmalade
and as I fear, she forgets every vowel.
How come I hadn't noticed she has stopped
painting her nails red, wearing longer skirts
again? Left, right, left, right, left, right, left, skip.
I wish I had a gun.

She stops outside Cheeky's Patisserie
to feed her green eyes on expensive cake,
I calculate calories, watch her face.
Where does she find that heartless conviction
the power it takes to keep her mouth shut?
Where the hell does she lock all that damage?
She kneels to be closer to them, I look
down at the nearly perfect blonde parting,
think of rotting roots, cruel soil, potential.
I wish I had a gun.

Then I'm stunned by the delicious waitress,
how her frail waist hums amongst the tables
of scorched Welsh accents, squabbling tourists
daring each other to 'go for doughnuts'.
A sweat patch under a brunette's left breast
reminds me of that stupid holiday...
'the cheap deal to happy ever after'
the tender skin and sticky tequilas,
a beach somewhere that began with a G.
I wish I had a gun.

# HEADACHE

It is precise.
A malignant art
that chews me
like a jealous twin.

It is immaculate.
A wasp kissing
its own sting
exact as nothing is.

# HEIRLOOM

*(for John O'Donaghue)*


While I swelled my mother's belly
a tumour helped itself to her,
I was born premature
an hour before she died.

I've come to know her through avoided questions,
overheard conversations, Uncle Eamon's moods,
as the woman who wore black and white stripes
and ate grey ice cream in her honeymoon photos.

She's the blackthorn rosary that dad gave me
on my twenty-first birthday in a simple box,
the christening shawl she had crocheted
and folded in tissue like a prayer;

It smelt of imagined lavender,
a gentle mess of untamed wool
that Dad wrapped my violet child in
when the white coffin arrived.

# HIDDEN THINGS

I have sat here on Tuesday afternoon for years,
watched her rock, mumble and nap among keepsakes
that trace her life like forgiven scars.

I have often wondered but never asked
about the unframed cross-stitch of three raw roses
clenched tight as a jaw, sealed with a cotton kiss

that she nests in four generations of photographs
as if hiding it among friends and relatives
to protect it from the sun like a fresh baby.

I am intrigued by her hidden things
since she started slurring, losing interest
in the weather, forgetting to comb her hair.

I am especially fond of the crooked china plate
camouflaged by complicated wallpaper
and black hearts that lurk in the scarlet tulips

she has delivered from the Scilly Isles
fortnightly. She keeps her secrets safe, locked,
encrypted in this scramble of ornaments.

We used to discuss politics, nonsense, God
until her chiselled wit lost its purchase
and so now the soft tick-tocking clock,

and the view across the park
are company enough when I watch her
rock, mumble and nap among keepsakes.

# HOTEL

we meet in room 101
at the same time
every week

the ensuite is a scream
of lemon and lime tiles
the toilet is terrified white

you cling to nicotine
blow smoke rings:
ochre halos in my hair

as we fumble-speak
like clumsy cousins
and the mirror glares

at our unstitched sex
watching us fail
to fake ourselves

as we fail to escape
in this hundred square feet
of woodchip and veneer

where creases gossip
in off-white cotton
and our awkward shadow

crawls backward up the wall

# ITALY

On the balcony under sallow light
I hear a viscous scream to the left
of outside, imagine high heels, a broken

smile, an end. Italy has changed too much
or perhaps I haven't changed enough?
I remember the intermittent summers

spent here scavenging for a head start,
an emergency exit out of the every days
stacked into a slow lifetime in Brighton.

But now the mosaic tiled aisle:
St Martin walking toward the altar
hand in hand with a crippled child

hardly matter.

# JACK'S CAFF

I sit in the hum
of second hand conversation
drinking powdered coffee
from a Spice Girls mug
watching the world go round
backwards.

Condensation makes it look
like the windows are sweating
outside the high street is fizzing
as the maze of undone top buttons
escape another day of beige décor
and air conditioning.

In Jack's caff the oblivious waitress
waits in a chip fat tea stained apron
for a lady with a spam coloured rinse
to count out a fist of loose change
onto the red formica counter
to save her breaking into a fiver.

Huddled in a corner behind the door
a blonde gang of cheap makeup
pull adolescence out of shape
flirt with Cosmopolitan and dream
of being fondled in places
they haven't yet found for themselves.

Opposite them an animal rights activist
hides behind a rash of acne
and bloodstained badges
scoffing veggie breakfast
fried in sarcastic lard.
The waitress grins —

watching him shovelling
greasy moss and compost
'cos she knows he's ogling
undressing the giggling skirts
frying slices of their pale thighs
in his eyes again.

To the left of the loo
a too young high-heeled mum
rams a screaming pram
and over-budget carrier bag
smack into the ankles
of a silver spooned future –

tarnished by a father
who left his quick signature
in her knickers at a dark party.
Behind her a fuss of students
in Oxfam duffle coats
bunch like terrorists

around salt and pepper pots
planning another revolution
getting their head around Marxism
as dictated by a corduroy jacket
that can't convince its own
argument anymore.

Next to the fire exit
a nest of squawking kids
pool pocket money
in a grubby saucer
to buy a milkshake
that gives their age away

they suck synthetic strawberry
through striped plastic
and flash a B&H snatched
from a mum's handbag

as bad habit's already
having its collar felt.

In the window seat a brood
of strapping young navvies
with broad Dublin accents
fill their crusty Doc Martens
with full English breakfasts.

I think of the famine.

# JAYWALKING

My blade jaywalks across canvas,
bullies red to bleed to the edge

then it drags blue back
into a whirlpool of purples

and I wade through the mistakes
that colour makes.

Sometimes I sketch the high street
through my big window,

where the real world tick-
tocks in short skirts and t-shirts.

I stopped painting yellow
on the day that undid Jack

in a simple accident
that a child could manage —

the day his mother started to clip
the ends off sentences

bevelling her Dublin accent
as if apologising for the space it takes.

I paint purple for her
force red into blue

like blood and bruises.

# JILTED BOUQUET

This town is a featureless portrait

of souls welded to bus stops
waiting... waiting for later

stapled to aggressive denim
and ribbon thin lycra killing

time. Killing time under
the seamless smoke ring

that squirms from the pit chimney
wild and thick as a gypsy's beard.

Poison has pulled the sky
out of shape and left a chain

of broken girls to tout flesh
for black confetti and jilted bouquets.

# KAISERSTRASSE

*(for Michael Donaghy)*

Heat has kidnapped the attic. Vindictive.
Janis Joplin is bouncing off the walls,
his eyes close as he waits for the needle
to back-flip that chorus in scratched vinyl:
make me feel like a natural woman
make me feel like a natural woman
lyrics that drag him back to Jade's bed-sit:
her vodka-temper, widowed lingerie,
Klimt prints, bitten kisses, wounded music.
Standing on the balcony he throws three
wishes at tarmac, hopes she's been blinded,
that her sleep aches and he still stains her sheets.
He needs mangled hotel rooms now, raw prayer.
The stubborn view of Berlin, simmering.

# KING PIN
*(for Jan Goodey)*

He was god:

Oxblood 18 hole
steel toe capped
Doc Martens

skin-fit bleach jeans
khaki Harrington
starched Ben Sherman.

He was suede shaven
a flee-run running
temple to nape

an Indian ink
*cut here* tattoo
across his neck

a silver ring in his top lip
a chipped front tooth:
He was a Cocky Fuck.

The handsome King
in a scrambled gang
of harmless lads

who used to crash
round the garages
getting wasted

on Thunderbird
cider spliff and glue.
He used to sniff until

he could taste blood

'til his shadow started
arguing back in backwards —

his broken head pressed
against an untuned radio
moaning two-tone into one

note.
I kissed him once at Steve's 18th
out of my tree on Benylin and sherry.

He cracked my lipstick
his relentless erection
pressed against my left thigh.

He tasted like a deep breath
in my father's shed
or the sixth form art room

where my lovesick compass
engraved his name in my desk.
I loved him in spite of good advice

because he dared me to let him stare into my eyes.

# LEAVING JOHN

I hired Stan Jones (& son)
their blue van, a Tuesday afternoon
to move nine years in April
to a one bedroom flat
a number five bus ride away.

Stan wore a black fingernail,
a beer-gut-stretched T-shirt
stained by the poll tax riots he still fights
with sixth form politics as if holding on
to someone he never really was.

Now I don't recognise the life
I've packed into boxes and labelled too neat:
Keep Upright, Breakable, Handle with Care.
(Stan has no idea I'm leaving a husband…
polite conversation doesn't ask).

Moving was Marion L Spencer's choice,
I imagine her naked too often:
stockings, Chanel flesh, green eyes
kissing John's midlife crisis goodnight
in expense paid rooms.

I pretend to be interested in Stan's new girlfriend:
a redhead, loves curry, three kids,
then he grunts for the choc-chip biscuits
he finished a milky three heaped spoons ago
and that image back flips back in:

Marion's earring in my washing machine. Typical. Gold.

# LEGACY

Life has taught us not to bother
with each other's trivia,

but sometimes at bus stops,
at supermarket checkouts

or when weather becomes
suddenly significant

I miss you.

The smell of your pillow,
the heartless violet scar

tucked behind your ear
and wonder if you ever think

of that power cut, the spilt milk
the stain we never forgave.

Sometimes, I drink Sapphire gin
on purpose to remind myself

why lemons and cinnamon exist
and look at those photographs,

tug my memory like a bully
but your legacy will always be

that drizzly Sunday in bed
listening to Sinatra,

dropping crumbs.

# LOOK

I look at the space
I take until I can almost see

the vacancy that is
not me.

# MENU

Eeezy- peezy-lemon-squeezy days
when we all 'catlicked'
in the kitchen sink

and Mum hummed Sinatra
while rinsing my hair
with Dad's big mug.

Monday was usually
a fist of mashed spuds
and knuckle of salty butter

that bled pale yellow lava
into a spam fritter and beans.
Tuesday was tinned red soup

with a doorstep then red jelly.
Wednesday and Thursday
was a 'Mum's clever pie' but

Friday's tea didn't need a plate!
That fizzy-sniff of fish and chips
snuggled in proper newspaper,

the utterness of vinegar
and Dad's pickled egg
that never made sense.

My uncertainty of gherkins.

# NOVEMBER

November is nursing my weathered eye
so staring through the shallow horizon
I will this spiteful winter to subside.

The relentless grey has rendered me blind
and I crave the memory of cloud-cotton.
November is nursing my weathered eye

and no matter how hard the view may try
it can not comfort a storm with reason.
I will this spiteful winter to subside

so as the carnage can not be denied:
the damage abandoned by late autumn.
November is nursing my weathered eye

and the sun half-hides like a guilty spy
as frozen bullets bludgeon the season.
I will this spiteful winter to subside

and lend the aching sky to kinder light:
let weather undress like a chameleon.
November is nursing my weathered eye.
I will this spiteful winter to subside.

# ODD

A man with a chiselled wife
handed me a cream envelope
at the bus stop I use after work.

The address, written in mauve pencil
(which seemed odd for some reason)
was on the other side of London.

He said there was no need to rush
and apologised for not escorting me but
he was up to his neck in sky.

He admitted he had watched me,
liked the way that I waited,
knew I was born for the job.

I didn't wonder why
this cut-out couple didn't
have their own chauffeur,

ignored the touting cabs,
or were in Hackney at all?
I just adored their dead-end-ness

found their lack a strange comfort
so took their kind firework
without a word.

# ON THE RANCH

Estelle welcomes me with a generous neckline,
flirts like pollen, knows how to tease *the slow blood*

I catch a snap of scarlet bra strap bitten flesh
brave lingerie that fails to tame her monstrous breasts
that quiver like rubber puddles when she giggles at my jokes.

I swell at the promise her cheeky hemline makes,
the thong that cuts into her fat arse leaving its mark
in the black satin skirt that clings to her like rain.

I love this meadow of pretty weeds
this shameless oasis where Estelle sells her smile
and attention to me.

# ONCE UPON AN AUTUMN

It began once upon an autumn.

She's kept the crisp linen napkin
from their first date
in a crimson restaurant

a silver coffee shop spoon
from a fairy tale weekend
in a hotel with a French accent

twenty-nine beer mats
from twenty nine Sunday lunches
in a cosy rose-rimmed pub

and a vanity bag of corks
pulled on special occasions
that she's forgotten. Now

she lends him skin to pay
for the apologetic bouquets
he buys from the corner shop –

bunches of colour tamed
and suffocated in cellophane –
double knotted at the neck

with gaudy nylon bows
that she rips with her teeth
over the kitchen sink.

He has taught her
how to hate properly
how to bleed on demand

how to watch mascara run
in a locked bathroom
how to hunt slowly

and master patience exactly
like an anorexic kneeling
at a midnight fridge.

# ONCE

If you kiss me twice,
I will tell you once

again.
I am a spiteful cat lurking

I hunt footprints
in puddles,

is my brittle-eye, a curse
or a blessing? Honestly...

She can not love you
    if she can't smell me.

# PARTY

I stayed to hide inside the party
to watch the space

between things happening;
stared into brutal music

asked anonymous lyrics to explain.
Tried too hard to fancy the pseudo-someone

with a fluorescent Mohican,
his girlfriend, my chances.

I left when there was nowhere to go
and fumbled home up the King's Road

in a yesterday-dress and bare feet
chastised by October frost.

A van, two vans and an S reg
passed at dawn speed

as each streetlight spluttered,
off.

# PATIENCE

An unread bible
another hotel room
trivial as logic.

Here is that moment
again when silence bites
behind my teeth... baiting

patience.

I wait for you slowly
to press your fingerprints
into me like benign thorns

as I count the backs
of your teeth
with my tongue.

You spell French
prayers incorrectly
through my hair

then across my forehead
then bless my eyelids
backwards.

We watch our stare
fight in mid air
as we stand face to face

like brave things.

# PIROUETTE

We concoct supple danger
in a Chelsea wine bar

where wounded jazz
fractures the baby grand.

We play intricate games
like preened rats

leave scenarios poised
eager to dive like blades

from the tips of our tongues
as we play with breath but

I stop
when you dare me

to pirouette closer to the edge
where indelicate waits patiently.

And instead I imagine tracing
neat gin around your lips

with a Japanese paint brush
or the subtle flavour of a blush.

# POLAROID

I still dread August
remember the white cotton
holidays spent at Uncle Fred's

how he watched my hips happen
over the years, soft-prodded
my nipples with the pad of his thumb

they swell pinker and plumper
every summer he'd whisper
unbuttoning them clumsily

I still dread August.
Still stick pins into the black
and white Polaroid

where Aunty Pam forced me
to stand, poised like thunder
under a ridiculous tree.

# POSH COFFEE

I've just returned from another plastic chat

at the café you call mutual territory
where we chase different clichés
round the same circle over posh coffee.

Today I told thin air I can't pretend again
and won't pick up the phone
when 2am tells me it's you.

My hall is yellow, chaos
lots of lots of, crafty mess,
the carpet doesn't match itself —

off cuts, the exercise bike has given up
and the cupboard won't shut —
a hive of photos and notebooks gossiping.

The living room sulks against the east wall
it is a moody room that locks me out
when temper slams it. It is locked.

I try to amuse the handle but
it is locked so I stand outside
its frosty glass like a truant

tamed by the moment
this lends me to think
twice. Then the sudden pulse

of a manic ambulance rips
London Road in half and puts
my distress into perspective

so I reach for a paperclip
from the tub of bits
I keep next to the phone

to make me feel efficient
pull it into mischief with my teeth
tease the keyhole 'til it forgives me

The room is full of afternoon
the spider plant that tries to die
hangs above smug bookshelves

titles with bad attitudes
grind the same axe
amongst themselves

and smuggled among
chewed novels the bible
hides like a spy

the sofa rests in leftover sun
I surrender in its warm arms
fish for trivia in yesterday's paper

until the headline
'STOP BEFORE IT'S TOO LATE'
baits my eye like a crooked smile:

another chic victim
of the addiction that is killing you
too slowly.

# QUARRY TILES

He's spilt her on the kitchen floor
she lies curled toward the sun
watching the warm leak
from her temple crawl
toward the door like a fat worm.

He goes upstairs to change his shirt
leaving her to count the ninety-eight
stripes in the curtain again
the hem still needs mending
she'll get some red cotton tomorrow.

She hears the cough
phlegm-spit-in-the-toilet, flush –
knows he'll be back in twenty-seven steps
to smoke a Marlboro to the filter
sink another Tennants Extra then

fuck off anywhere.
When he leaves she'll drink tea
with dirty breakfast things,
get dressed, mop up the mess
before the kids get in from school.

# RANDOM

The scenario chases its tail
around my mind like a blind stallion —
why did I agree to coffee then
go Dutch on a bottle of whiskey
and a fistful of random flavoured crisps
as we giggled home arm in arm
past the off licence on Baker street?

# REDUNDANT

I eat tuna from a tin,
watch London Road
fuelling tempers,
wonder what the green car
had for breakfast.
Why I care.

Through a must-wash window
the 5a throws up into the bus stop
then moans on and on
to the same feng shui beige office blocks
and chrome shops as every day
at approximately 8:06.

The kettle clicks:
another day begins,
without me.

# REEK

As I move closer
to comb her hair

candy floss white
candy floss frail

the reek of warm piss
tears my heart

more than any love
I have ever lost.

# REVENGE

*(dedicated to p.m.s)*

I'm going to scratch my name in Arabic
across the bonnet of your dad's metallic Lexus.
I saw it parked outside his fat house
like a sticky kid poking its tongue out
when I took the long route to Sainsbury's
to buy marzipan and tampons
last Wednesday afternoon.
I'll use the Yale key you left
propped against the clock
with the unopened envelope

addressed to 'us' from Nat West
then I'll patrol his cat flap
like a psychotic bitch on heat
and kidnap your *precious pussy*,
lure her with the fishy titbits
I still find down the sofa,
I never trusted her eyes.
She's a fat ginger bag of scabs
that scratches at her bald patch
leaves abstract blood sketches
across the worktops and walls

stains your lap like a mistress.

I hated the scraps of warm mouse
I used to find in my socks,
the headless pigeons in the laundry bin
lurking, unexpected like bailiffs.
Yes, her last supper will be tuna
marinated in my piss and spit
before I boil her in a pair of my nan's
*American tan* nylons and then leave it
to cool on your bulimic sister's door step
so that she'll trip over it, into the rose beds

on her way to buy chocolate.

# ROADSIDE ROSES

He buys her time
with roadside roses
and guilt trips

looking for himself
in the broken promises
he leaves for her to pluck.

He doesn't notice:
she hasn't worn weekday lipstick
since the stitches dissolved...

dissolved like the sugar lumps
she watches drown in coffee shop
spoons where she sits for hours,

safe among the trivial strangers
she trusts more than herself.
There she presses tenderness,

teases the fresh bruises
that turned indigo overnight,
while she lays awake,

raw as a butcher's window,
blooding cotton like a virgin,
keeping their little secret under the bed.

# ROSEWOOD

I've put a deposit on the rosewood bureau
that's been sulking under months of dust
in the antique shop window.

It will take me nineteen Mondays to buy it
out of misery and welcome it to the scrabble
of other impractical furniture I've bought slowly,

to introduce it to the colours smells and sounds
my life makes, then I'll stand it against the wall
like a soldier praying for bullets.

# SAME JEANS

It can't still be Tuesday
these the same jeans

scuffed magazines
polystyrene cups.

Until the accident
sacred had been

that after sex thing
a weekend lie in

the soft thud of dropping
off a bellyful of Friday night.

But now standing
on the wrong side

of toughened glass
he watches her small breath

and knows that sacred
is the place

between the drips
drip feeding her

and him.

# SECOND HAND

I burgle stubs of chit-chat
left on buses and trains,

scribble invented names
in the margins of notebooks

practice strangers' signatures
on the backs of envelopes.

I steal details;
like the blonde hook of hair

that nestles in the nape
that I sit behind in church,

the bookmark I found at Clapham:
green capital lettering spelling 'Jacq'

I imagine a muscular mind, cold
a spinster's heart.

# SICKLY PINK

Every night the nicotine-nurse
who sucks unconvincing mints
pulls the sickly pink floral print
curtains into chinks.

Every night at eight-thirty
she plants me in a nightie
and I crave the privacy
my body's lost in cold hands.

Every night she counts
a white pill into a plastic pot
pours water from a jug
put back out of reach

and leaves the dark to help itself.

# SLITHER

Kiss me like anaesthesia —
let's foster the moment
slow dancing makes

take me somewhere stupid,
pretend it makes a difference
for as long as it takes.

Please, call me Madeleine,
it will make things easier
when we bend the curve

when we juggle blades
and hunt for the soft place
our fingers can still smell

when we gloss over the mess
that life makes hushing scars
begging each other

for one more sliver of fear.

# SMILE

We shared a roll up,

watched the sun rise in a striking match
toasted dawns chorus with ouzo in egg cups
on the back step of your best mate's house.

We revelled in the stun of Marillion lyrics
compiled a list of green things
until we ran out of fingers.

You introduced me to Max Ernst
and Amsterdam, I watched your jaw bone
as you spoke but never heard a word.

We had Catholicism and inertia in common,
fed each other random jokes, plans, details
and trivia both famished for words.

Then you stood up, jutted your right hip out
left a quick kiss on the crown of my head,
told me to wait, to count down from ten

and skipped up the hallway singing
*'we gotta get out of this place if
it's the last thing we ever do.'*

I sat astonishingly still, eyes shut
'til my mind went China-white
and I couldn't feel my heart beat.

My gut was a jazz of starlings
as you handed me a crash helmet,
and watched me fall a little in love.

We escaped the estate
went to places beyond bus stops
your wing mirror a flash-flood

of snapshots: bright country lanes
in the swerve of apricot clouds
we left, flailing behind us.

I dragged my cheek across
your cracked black leather jacket
collected scratches, scars, souvenirs.

We had breakfast at a kebab van,
you told the fat Greek man
that we were on honeymoon,

had eloped from Gretna Green
he laughed and wished us luck
(I wondered if he got the joke)

Over the years life has proven
there is no such thing as *certain*
except that one April morning in '85

will always make me smile inside.

# SOBER

I am dead of water
so the half glass

of drunk beckons
like a stocking top

as the restraint
that I nurse

like a grey baby
aches and regret

takes the glass
by the neck

threatening
that moment when

nearly is too close.

# SOFT FENCE

The party was a soft fence against the weather.

In the corner an army of Stella stood to attention
unopened, watching the war –

the slaughter of bottles and cans crushed
and abandoned like one night stands.

In the hall small talk fought with stubborn music
I tried to unlace a ginger conversation but when

he offered me a cigarette I wanted
to be the someone who wasn't scared of

smoking it
again.

Against the kitchen wall a brittle couple fucked
like spastic ballerinas, the plain girl grunting

politely as he threw himself into her
aimlessly.

I watched his bared teeth and thought
of a fish spine snapped by a rapid hand,

the mess a hook makes of a throat,
the secret that was melting in my mouth.

Yes the party was a soft fence but I knew
the weather will always wait.

A patient wolf.

# SOLEMN

I am here to book fun in eight months away.

Across the manic carpet
behind a restless desk
a plump twenty-something
agitates PC keys.

I flick through magazines
of pristine everywheres
I've never been
never met in an atlas
or at party chit-chat

On page six –

A vanilla beach, a flesh circus
of six packs and unwrapped breasts
tassels of lean bikinis stretched and
tenderised by salt water simmer
under a pantomime sky

On page nine –

a love drunk couple sip chilled fizz
and beam at their symmetrical children
watching them chase melting ice cream
through fumbling fingers past wrists
across palms and down arms

with giggling tongues.
in the distance a toned teenager
throws a rainbow beach ball
across a staple onto the next page
where his girlfriend waits on tiptoe.

Impossible colours spill through the brochure
into European cities where sophists graze
on newspapers at pavement cafés
and greedy tourists with spiteful cameras
bite lumps out of the architecture

I continue browsing a world away
until a raincoat with a wet wife
coughs and I stop at page twenty-eight
where a solemn mountain suffocates
under a mistake that the snow has made.

# STILL LIFE

Since I stopped juggling water
its easier to swallow, spit
chastise my appetite with a cigarette.

Anna tells me I am provocative
as a broken jaw when I sit monk-still,
naked and feral in her shivering studio

where a Russian radio faces the wall,
dirty-water-jam-jars mutter and the tap
drips into unwashed mugs and spoons.

I am stunned by her careless beauty
in this mess of gossiping curios,
immaculate details, broken things

where canvases hang, sit and stand
at indifferent angles. Anna's breath
is an Aspirin plume in this bitter place.

She reinvents me every week –
oil, pastel, charcoal, ink
each stroke surgeon-soft,

she tells me to stop looking
for the moon in my handbag
and we laugh just enough.

But I can still smell blue cheese –
aggravating the fridge that night
he unpacked his temper and left

the past                    ajar
no matter how carefully
she paints over the cracks.

# STILL

Life woke up late again,
laid perfectly still and stared
into each inch of ceiling

listened to manic traffic
that stilled summer
like smart wasps

watched the afternoon tiptoe
across the room indifferently.
Everything was still Tuesday.

Rachel's advice
still didn't make sense:
exercise green veg, fresh air.

Rachel hasn't called since...
but still sends a lemon rose
hand-wrapped in white tissue

on special occasions,
from the florists in Bastille Street
that smells of adultery.

The letter from Japan still hasn't come
but every day junk mail
waits like conscience,

creeping in with the manila bills
at that still-time just before
a day begins, to smell.

# SURRENDER

The sky is a menace of vultures
circling like paranoia overhead,

autumns starving oaks and cedars
buckle like my mothers knuckles –

branches sketch charcoal profiles
across deaf clouds that swell rain.

I sense her at my shoulder again,
humming broken songs...

the widow, draping profound shadows
as November makes its last request.

The opaque moon proffers a shy light
seducing the view like a grinning tumour.

Summer, now sucked senseless
as auburn and amber leaves surrender,

and tall trees cower under threadbare
veils of frost.

Winter flexes its fist in the forest,
I shiver in thin wool.

# TAINTED LOVE

I'm like a child looking for Santa
in a frosted window, as if I've died
but God has forgotten to tell me.

Lying under the damp patch –
the shape of Italy sinks
into magnolia woodchip.

Upstairs the student lovers
fuck-bruise the headboard again,
he plays chaotic psychedelia

when she visits at weekends,
listens to Leonard Cohen
on headphones when alone.

He's a moody-groomed bed-head
she's an elfin in pink Doc Martens
laddered black stockings, losing weight

I hear her moan on cue then,
wait for the hush then,
smile to myself then,

think twice about getting up.

# TANGERINE

Monday, five months of texts agreed we should
rendezvous in a lay-by. You left a
marriage at home, I wore nervous perfume
and your favourite colour, hoped it might
remind you of Austria, tequila,
the backseat of Darren's Cortina, how
in love we thought we were. It is Friday
now and I sit in Sainsbury's car park,

play with matches, rewind, count backwards from
one hundred in French and back again. Yes,
I could text, apologise, make a joke
of it, deny I listen to Lloyd Cole
deliberately but... You shouldn't have
kissed me. I shouldn't have worn tangerine.

# TASTE

From a teased distance
he pays immaculate attention
to the blonde shadows
he peels for perfume.

His grin is keen as hurt
a buckled skull bone-shaven
a dead straight navy hairline
one malicious scar.

He rents himself
when he feels contemptuous
milks stale strangers
remembers the taste.

# THANK YOU

Old Holborn has left her provocative ghost,
an overcast of grey chiffon, ribbon.

She will fade, take her seductive hem but
know when, to leave the odd cough

at the back of my throat to remind me
that you are in other company now.

Someone else who cherishes the stink
of you lurking in her hair on the bus,

who hunts her towels for the sudden whiff
of you left incidentally. Someone else who

doesn't wash until you bring her
your next dose of skin, your forgiven grin.

But we are killing us too slowly my love
and so I call a truce, I'm leaving the room.

Thank you from the colour of my blood
for the stuff like asking me 'what if'

when you stood at the edge
of Beachy Head in that edible storm.

For letting me drive there in the dark
with your headlights off.

# THE COAST ROAD

He stopped taking the coast road
when her cataracts got stuck in his throat

and his answers got lost
in her ridiculous questions.

When she forgot to giggle every time
they passed The King's Head

and her coy smile couldn't find him
in Asda. When the simple meals started.

When she began to pluck at food
like a broken bird

and *sad* tripped him up in public
for the second time in his life.

But he's learning how to field
her seamless moods,

where to stop trying,
when to leave the room.

When to hold her when she needs him most
and let go when he needs her more.

# THE INTERVIEW

The receptionist is anorexic

has a hint of hip
rhubarb cheeks:
a blonde ghost that digs
itself out of its own throat.

The office is serious

an oxblood Chesterfield
mahogany bookcase
leather-bound classics
a gabardine man with olive eyes.

I wear snakeskin sling backs

to exaggerate my negligible ankles
translucent seamed stockings,
ivory silk fitted blouse
pearl button at the neck

and sit

teasing the nipple
of my suspender belt
through rouge cashmere
I never do

wear knickers to interviews.

# THE REASON FOR THURSDAYS

I paint my nails an uncomfortable colour
and wear complicated underwear on Thursdays.

I work at an office in a nest of cheap body sprays,
oily humour, ill fitting bras and smokers coughs.

I was parked here by a break-down 4 years ago
at the furthest desk from the window, but still can't

risk the view. Every morning I watch Fat-John
digress by the coffee machine peeling gossip

and making up drunken fights out with the lads
and one night stands with girls he'll never smell.

Pat (the senior clerk) digs her words
out of a stubborn Manchester accent

and in spite of the weather
is always unbuttoned

two buttons too much
so as her crinkled cleavage can breathe

as it suffocates the gold plate gate chain
that spits back the florescent light.

But on Thursdays Mr Elviane's black attaché
walks past my desk at the same steady steady pace

leaving a graze of insistent aftershave
on his way to the deli on St James Street

where he orders bespoke sandwiches
sips black bitterness, smokes Turkish cigarettes

and flirts with the sallow waitress
with a chestnut ponytail and soft hips.

I hang my week on Thursdays, they solve
the ache that I nurse like a sin.

# THE RIM

Today has been waiting
since we started pulling
wings off things,

hunting ugliness
like dirty kids
we wanted this.

To covet each other
like cheap souvenirs
cracking patiently.

But now I run
my finger round the rim
in some attempt to find

where things end. And begin.

# THICKER THAN WATER

The heel of my silk ballet pump
is blood-stained already

we haven't even left the house.
Maria is reed slim, skin to shame fruit.

I asked her not to ask me this time,
I didn't want to be her bridesmaid again.

I am too tall for the front line
too self obsessed to fuss over

the waddle of flower girls' honey curls
cinnamon ribbons snots and snails.

The best man looks like a TDA
that's been abandoned in a lay-by

and the groom...scrubbed up well
after our sex and breakfast in bed

before the carnations arrived.

# THIN CURTAIN

I went to bed early last night
with the Sellotaped spine paperback
I underline in green,
(scribble in the margins
as if coaxing something out.)

Our unmade bedroom smelt of excuses
and kicked-off shoes, so I lit an incense stick
and traced the lazy shape smoke makes falling
between the cracks of our mix-n-match furniture
cluttered with the 'us' between you and me:

mug rings, bits and bobs of somethings
the uncertain clock broken by an argument,
the contents of your emptied pocket;
sixteen pence in loose change, wallet, keys,
and today's till receipt from Sainsbury's
for the usual: egg roll, cherry coke, King Size Twix.

I went to bed early last night
leaving you to grope the evening
for stimulating company on your own:
late night B-rate pornography
and blended whiskey again.

You trip-tip-toed in late.
I feigned sleep to avoid another faked headache
and watched you undress in the dim street light
that sneaks in through our thin curtain
that can't hide either side anymore.

# THIS ROOM

If I sit at that angle
it's nearly comfortable

but I fail when
you decipher my smile,

the crack it makes
across my face.

I am a tower of ash
in a sorry wind

when you hold me,
when we pretend

to be just friends
as we kiss cheeks

and I leave this room.
These corners, these stains,

this wallpaper cage
that watched us —

two cowards scared
of love out loud...

where you shuffled me like music,
steered my strings with clever wrists

nursed me with white noise
and the thud of your pulse

and I utterly miss this room
when I am everywhere else.

Snared in some handsome gaze,
held too close by another shirt

a pattern that,
I don't understand.

# TRAPS

The bus pulls away from Churchill Square. Rain
distorts the city seeming to stretch it like bubble gum
across the windscreen.

Every drop traps all the colours of North Street
in it, jumbles them up into balls of rainbow
that cling to the glass until they don't.

We get stuck in the every day rush hour traffic
and Christ my temper aches as a wisp of baby
inflicts its malicious chorus on us all.

I really want to scream back in its small face,
so what if it's hungry, so what if it's wet
just like me?

Is its scrawny young mum really so numbed,
so sucked inside out that she's given up
trying to find a quite place in life?

Its mouth is no bigger than a penny
yet when its plump lips peel back
to free another gummy scream

it becomes a raw trap
that I wouldn't trust my finger in.
Again, the bald diva demands an encore

the same verse over and over and then
a stupid fat passenger pampers it
with a smile. Red rag to the Bull.

The tiny terrorist grinds its eyelids,
holds a few tears back, hostages,
cute bullets to threaten mummy with

in the middle of the night.

# VAMPIRE TIME

The smell of rose petals and petrol

swell this anonymous place.
You adjust the blindfold slightly
command me kindly to take your arm

rest your hand over mine
and begin to walk at a safe pace.
Undressed, my feet sink delighted

into carpet that is soft as blunt grass.
The mellow thud in my chest
takes a deep breath and

I offer myself to your promise
to show me who I really am
If I lend you trust.

In the comfort of blindness
I let my imagination
curl its tail around the corridors

as I'm led toward the loose-hipped sound
of a solo saxophone, painless music for the ghosts
I imagine making love under the muscular furniture

that I am sure must live here in your kingdom
with waxed antiques polished and creaking
in this mascara black.

You stop.

Remove the blindfold and turn me slowly
to face the wall where an abstract portrait
of a bald girl stares at me like an accusation.

*Terrified I spin into an endless mirror opposite*
*that hooks me into my own eyes.*
*They are ripe, I am ready to pounce.*

# VINTAGE

I bought an antique teacup
from a secondhand shop

the old woman wrapped it
in a month-ago newspaper

already magnolia edged
in our mutual attempt

to keep history in its place.

# VODKA AND VALIUM

Liam didn't stir,
snug among the curls in his cot
unaware the day had cracked

downstairs I heard
Mum and Auntie Kathleen
fumbling with sympathy

it felt just like the morning
Uncle Sean got out of prison,
moved in, kipped on the sofa

smoked skinny roll-ups
and swigged stout
in the green chair all day.

I got up, cold lino,
my breath swelled uncertain
in the too early air.

I took each stair suspiciously
as if hunting Santa and saw Mum
through the banister rails trying to cry.

She shouted 'hey, go and get a cigarette
to steady me nerves,' so I did;
Piccadilly untipped, the bitter pinch

of baccy on my tongue,
that first blunt lug,
I put the kettle on.

Dad came down, bare feet and string vest
dragging unfinished sleep
and a fug of Old Holborn

Mum said Uncle Damien was found
in a Jury's hotel room:
vodka and valium.

Mum said it was a blessing,
Dad said nothing, just coughed,
phoned work, rolled another smoke.

# WHITE INK

He was the reason for cravats

cuff links and pinkie rings,
wore green Italian leather shoes
and was everything vodka promised
to the right mood.

He was exactly handsome
and blurred our evening rehearsals
with a Portuguese wine
I mispronounced on purpose.

He swelled my dressing room
with Cuban cigar smoke,
a suggestion of cologne
and jokes about his double knotted wife.

He taught me the purpose of curtains,
how to bone a soliloquy till it fit on a cuff,
scratch a quote into my watchstrap with a compass,
and how to write a killer line in white ink

across my wrist.

# WHY

No one knows why
he hates Mozart so much

he tried to explain it once
to a shaving mirror

in a Premier Lodge
with a view of suburbia

but failed like a grey baby.

Photograph: Giya Makonda-Wills

BERNADETTE CREMIN has published three previous collections of poetry: *Perfect Mess* (Biscuit Publishing) *Speechless, Miming Silence* (Waterloo Press) and *Loose Ends* (Pighog Press). Her work has won various awards. Her one-woman show 'Altered Egos,' six poetic monologues depicting six untidy lives, was awarded Arts Council of England funding after being made runner-up Best Literary/Performance Piece at the Brighton Fringe Festival. Cremin has collaborated with musicians, filmmakers, scientists and photographers. Her first spoken-word CD, "Sensual Assassins", was released by State Art in 1998 and was followed in 2015 by a second spoken-word CD, "Guilty Fist". Her film work includes the film *Inside Skin*; and her photography work includes *Birth* and *Science (Promise or Threat)*. She also reads her work extensively in the UK and Ireland.